Beowulf

Text by
Gail Rae Rosensfit
(M.A., Hunter College)
Department of English
McKee Vocational Technical High School
Staten Island, New York

Illustrations by
Karen Pica

 Research & Education Association

What **MAXnotes**™ *Will Do for You*

This book is intended to help you absorb the essential contents and features of *Beowulf* and to help you gain a thorough understanding of the work. The book has been designed to do this more quickly and effectively than any other study guide.

For best results, this **MAXnotes** book should be used as a companion to the actual work, not instead of it. The interaction between the two will greatly benefit you.

To help you in your studies, this book presents the most up-to-date interpretations of every section of the actual work, followed by questions and fully explained answers that will enable you to analyze the material critically. The questions also will help you to test your understanding of the work and will prepare you for discussions and exams.

Meaningful illustrations are included to further enhance your understanding and enjoyment of the literary work. The illustrations are designed to place you into the mood and spirit of the work's settings.

The **MAXnotes** also include summaries, character lists, explanations of plot, and episode-by-episode analyses. A discussion of the work's historical context and language will help you put this literary piece into the proper perspective of what is taking place.

The use of this study guide will save you the hours of preparation time that would ordinarily be required to arrive at a complete grasp of this work of literature. You will be well prepared for classroom discussions, homework, and exams. The guidelines that are included for writing papers and reports on various topics will prepare you for any added work which may be assigned.

The **MAXnotes** will take your grades "to the max."

Dr. Max Fogiel
Program Director

Contents

> **Each episode includes List of Characters,**
> **Summary, Analysis, Study Questions and**
> **Answers, and Suggested Essay Topics.**

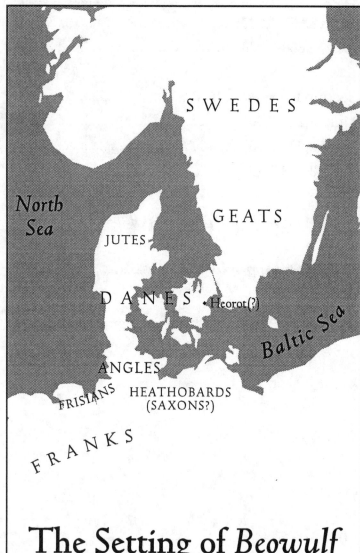

The Setting of *Beowulf*

Locations of tribes are necessarily vague

SECTION ONE

Introduction

The Poem

Very little is known about the origins of this 3,182–line Old
English poem. There is no known poet nor date of writing, although
various experts have suggested that it was written some time between 650 and 1,000 A.D. Only one manuscript survived Henry
VIII's dissolution of the monasteries (which included their librar-
ies, probably the only warehouses of writing at the time). Lawrence
Nowell, a sixteenth-century scholar, is sometimes credited with the
preservation of this manuscript since his name is written on one
of the folios. However, it is a copy with two distinctly different hand-
writings; it is not known if other copies exist nor how close to the
original this copy is. This sole manuscript has seriously deterio-
rated due to careless binding and a fire in 1731.

Two additional transcripts were made in 1786–7 by the Danish scholar Grimur Thorkelin, who was forced to guess at words or
lines missing because of this deterioration. This possibly epic
poem, with its long narrative of the deeds of a legendary figure sung
in an elevated style, was not titled until 1805 and first printed in
1815.

Historical Background

While the poem is Old English, it focuses on the Geats (a people
who lived in the southern part of Sweden before being conquered
by their traditional enemies, the Swedes, toward the end of the sixth
century) and Danes. Assumed to be composed sometime in the
eighth century A.D., it seems to accurately reflect Scandinavian

society and history of the sixth century A.D.; Higlac's raid of the Hathobards is historical fact.

The Angles, Saxons, and Jutes came to England from an area just below Denmark during the first great wave of Germanic migration in the fifth century when they were invited by Vortigen, king of the Britons, to help him repel the Picts and the Scots. Their easy victory and the fertile land they discovered led them to come in force, subjugating the Britons as they did. Once settled, they preserved the memories of their heroes using oral poetry, thereby keeping alive the ancient Germanic heroic code by which they lived.

This code included a rigid feudal system. The continuance of feuds and friendships established by fathers was expected of the next generation, although tribute was accepted as a means of concluding feuds and abolishing dishonor. The people were quite civilized and equally violent, being a warrior culture which valued courage the most and cowardice the least. Their chief was surrounded by companions who swore allegiance to him and would die in battle, rather than retreat (except to return), while the chief, in turn, was expected to perpetually prove his courage and generosity. The chief's greatest shame was to be outdone by either one of these companions or an enemy. As a rite of passage into manhood, once having proved their valor, the young men were publicly presented with spears and shields. If no battles presented themselves at home, the chief and his companions would go abroad to seek battles.

The reverence these people had for their women is demonstrated by their monogamy, and their acceptance of as close a bond between a man and his sister's son as that between father and son. Indeed, women were thought of as holy and possessing the gift of prophecy. A belief in Fate and foreseeing the future by casting lots were two other aspects of this warrior culture, despite the recent introduction of Christianity.

So new was Christianity that the Biblical references in the poem relate only to the Old Testament, while the poet seems to equate Fate and God's will. Grendel is regarded as the descendant of Cain, the first murderer whose story is told in the Old Testament, and the sword Beowulf uses to murder Grendel is decorated with depictions of the Old Testament's giants who were destroyed by the flood. The Christian poet writing the poem understood what these decorations are, but the pagan character viewing them did not. Nowhere in the poem is it suggested that Beowulf's death would be the first step in his immortality (in Heaven), and his body is burned upon the funeral pyre—a pagan custom. Accordingly, this culture is seen as embracing Christianity while admiring paganism.

While it is fairly commonly accepted that the author is a Christian, and possibly a monk, he used a pagan world as the setting for his poem. He is addressing a Christian audience, as is evidenced by the references to the Old Testament (mentioned in the previous paragraph) while telling the story of pagans, whom he seems to admire for firmly believing in and accepting a Higher Being which rules the world and men's actions much as the Christian God does. Beowulf himself is portrayed as a deeply religious pagan who offers thanks to this Higher Being, ascribes his strength to him, and even worries about having offended him. In some ways, this may be interpreted as a Christian typology (symbol for Christ) since he also attains virtue by strictly adhering to the old Germanic Code, which is not that dissimilar from the Christian Code. Much like Christ, this was Beowulf's way of life rather than an exercise in discipline. Beowulf, a pagan warrior, lived a life of kindness and non-condemnation even toward the soldiers who deserted him as he battled the dragon. In addition, both men lived lives of self-sacrifice, repeatedly risking and, ultimately, giving their lives for their people. While Beowulf may not have entertained the idea of offering salvation to his people, he was concerned with protecting them and, in so doing, did offer them a type of salvation. Christ may have done the reverse—concerned himself with his people's salvation while not necessarily thinking of himself as a protector and, in so doing, offering them a type of protection. However, it must be remembered that the Biblical references in the poem are to the Old Testament and Christ is not introduced until the New Testament, thereby raising some question as to whether or not Beowulf was intended as a Christian typology. Furthermore, unlike Christ, Beowulf actively seeks praise and glory.

Poetry of this period was recited, and more usually sung, at feasts, occasionally using the harp to keep the meter regimented.

Phrases were repeated to re-enforce the understanding of the events in the story and habitual phrases and epithets were part of the tradition and expected of the poets. This particular poem seems to have been meant for the feasts of kings and nobles. It may even have been created at such a feast based on the stories the singer (or "scop") had previously heard of the exploits of Beowulf, a possibly fictitious character. The audiences, also, would have been aware of their legendary history, myths, and stories, and have had some knowledge of the events mentioned in the poem via their cultural oral tradition. The Germanic people of the Dark Ages shared oral composition with Austria and northern France; the practice of this type of composition then traveled to Scandinavia and Iceland, employing a common body of narrative with the same heroes and incidences in widely separated times and places, but with the common appearance of the ethical principle of loyalty to another with vengeance for the breaking of this bond through cowardice or treachery.

Genre

This is a difficult poem to classify since it has no predecessors and nothing like it has survived. While usually considered an epic poem, Beowulf has also been labeled an elegy, perhaps for Beowulf himself or perhaps for the heroism of the past (and obviously admired by the Christian poet) pagan era. Others have felt it to be solely historical poetry about paganism.

One reason not to consider it an epic is that Beowulf has no specific tragic flaw which precipitates his downfall. He is an excellent, deeply religious, pagan warrior who does precisely what his culture expects of him—including seeking glory and protecting his people. Another reason is that it is longer than an epic, having three main episodes over a period of 50 years, rather than one event as is usual.

On the other hand, there is Beowulf as the epic hero who represents his culture and is noble, has considerable military prowess, and undying virtue. Several other elements of the epic poem are also evident in the poem: the lofty tone and style, the lengthy narrative, the genealogies, the involvement of the supernatural (in the form of the monsters, dragons, and giants), the invocation, and the voyage across the sea. Beowulf's battle in the dragon's underground lair may or may not be considered the obligatory trip to the underworld as found in the epic poem. While there are epic battles, they are not between universal champions, but rather between good and evil.

Master List of Characters

Geats:

Beowulf—*Higlac's follower and nephew by marriage; a great warrior; comes to Denmark with a band of 14 followers to help Hrothgar defeat Grendel since Hrothgar had ended a feud for Beowulf's father, Edgetho, when it threatened to cause war between the Geats and the Wulfings (a Germanic tribe); after the death of his king, Higlac, and Higlac's son, Herdred, was the Geat king for 50 years; also killed Grendel's mother; mortally wounded in battle with a third dragon when an old man.*

Edgetho—*Beowulf's father; married Hrethel's daughter, becoming Higlac's brother-in-law; fled to Hrothgar's Denmark after beginning a feud which resulted in his exile, since the people feared this feud would become a war.*

Efor—*Killed the Swedish king, Ongentho; given Higlac's daughter as a reward, making him Beowulf's cousin by marriage.*

Hathcyn—*Hrethel's son; accidentally killed his elder brother, Herbald, in a hunting accident which led to his father's dying of grief; became the Geat king with his brother, Higlac, upon Hrethel's death; killed in a battle with Sweden by the Swedish king, Ongentho.*

Herbald—*Eldest son of Hrethel; killed by his brother, Hathcyn, in a hunting accident.*

Herdred—*Son of Higlac; Geat king; killed by the Swedish king, Onela.*

Higd—*Higlac's wife.*

Higlac—*The young king of the Geats; married to Higd; Beowulf's uncle and lord; youngest son of Hrethel; father of Herdred; father-in-law to Efor; brother of Hathcyn and Herbald.*

Hondshew—*The young Geat soldier eaten by the monster, Grendel, in Herot (the hall built by the Danish king, Hrothgar, to house and celebrate his growing and victorious troops) during the first night the Geats sleep there when they arrive to conquer Grendel.*

Hrethel—*Father of Higlac, Hathcyn, and Herbald; married his daughter to Edgetho; Beowulf's grandfather; took Beowulf to live with him at age seven and loved him as a son; king of the Geats.*

Wiglaf—*Wexstan's son; a former Swede; the only soldier who accompanies Beowulf into his last and fatal battle with the dragon.*

Danes:

Beo—*Shild's son; Healfdane's father; became the Danish king upon Shild's death; long-reigning and popular king.*

Esher—*Hrothgar's closest friend and most trusted counselor; carried off by Grendel's mother (along with her son's claw) in retaliation for Grendel's death the first night the Danes return to Herot.*

Healfdane—*Son of Beo; father to Hergar, Hrothgar, Halga the good, and Yrs, who was married to the king of the Swedes, Onela.*

Hermod—*A Danish king who had ruled poorly and uncaringly, alienating his people.*

Hrothgar—*Son of Healfdane; builder of Herot; king of the Danes after his brother Hergar's death; ended Edgetho's feud; welcomed Beowulf and his band of 14 when they came to defeat Grendel; married to Welthow; father of Hrethric, Hrothmund, and Freaw (who married Ingeld).*

Shild—*Beo's father; Healfdane's grandfather; Hrothgar's great-grandfather; another long reigning, popular Danish king.*

Unferth—*Ecglaf's son; Hrothgar's courtier (attendant at the royal court); greets Beowulf joyfully when he arrives in Denmark but is afraid to join him in battling Grendel's mother; loans Beowulf Hrunting (his sword) to kill Grendel's mother.*

Welthow—*Hrothgar's queen.*

Others:

Dagref—*Killed Beowulf's lord, Higlac; was in turn killed by Beowulf.*

Finn—*Sung of as an example of bad character. He attacked his wife's people without warning, killing her son and brother. He was later murdered by enemies he had forced into a peace treaty.*

Grendel—*The monster who attacks Herot and murders Hrothgar's men, which results in Herot standing empty for twelve years; eats Hondshew the first night the Geats sleep in Herot; killed by Beowulf.*

Grendel's Mother—*Another monster; seeks revenge upon Beowulf for his having murdered her son; flees Herot when she sees she is losing the battle but takes her son's claw (which had been hanging on the wall as a trophy of his defeat) and Esher, Hrothgar's closest friend and advisor; eventually killed by Beowulf.*

Offa—*King of the Angles who did not migrate to what is now England, but rather stayed on the European continent.*

Onela—*Younger son of Ongentho; married to Healfdane's daughter; became the Swedish king by seizing the throne after his older brother's death; invaded the Geats to kill Herdred and the older of his two nephews who was heir to the Swedish throne; after returning home, permitted Beowulf to rule the Geats; killed by Beowulf during the invasion of Sweden by the surviving nephew.*

Ongentho—*The Swedish king who kills Hathcyn, the Geatish king and Hrethel's son, after Hrethel's death; killed by Higlac; Onela's father.*

Siegmund—*Successfully fought against a dragon, earning treasures; greatly glorified in the poems which were later sung.*

Wexstan—*Wiglaf's father; killed the older of Onela's nephews during the Swedish invasion of the Geats.*

Wulfgar—*A Swedish prince serving the Danish king, Hrothgar.*

Genealogies

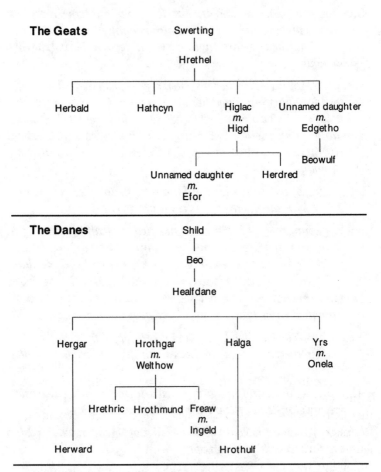

The Geats

Swerting
|
Hrethel
|
- Herbald
- Hathcyn
- Higlac *m.* Higd
- Unnamed daughter *m.* Edgetho — Beowulf

Higlac:
- Unnamed daughter *m.* Efor
- Herdred

The Danes

Shild
|
Beo
|
Healfdane
|
- Hergar — Herward
- Hrothgar *m.* Welthow
  - Hrethric
  - Hrothmund
  - Freaw *m.* Ingeld
- Halga — Hrothulf
- Yrs *m.* Onela

The Swedes

Ongentho
|
- Ohther
- Onela *m.* Yrs

Summary of the Poem

Hrothgar, the Danish king, builds a hall—Herot—for his brave soldiers. The first night they sleep there, Grendel—a monster—attacks and kills 30 of them. The attacks continue, keeping Herot empty and Hrothgar sorrowful for 12 years. Beowulf sails to Denmark with a band of 14 men to defeat the monster, since Hrothgar had saved Edgetho, Beowulf's father, from a feud which threatened to start a war years earlier.

The first night the Geats (Beowulf's people) sleep in Herot, Grendel strikes again. Hondshew, a young warrior, is killed in the attack. Beowulf fights with Grendel barehanded since Grendel bewitched the weapons, rendering them useless. Beowulf tears off the monster's claw, arm, and shoulder, mortally wounding him, although Grendel flees to his lair before dying. Hrothgar orders that Herot be cleansed and a feast prepared. He presents Beowulf with prizes of a golden banner, a helmet, a coat of mail, an ancient sword, and eight horses. Grendel's claw, arm, and shoulder are hung on the wall of Herot.

The Danes return to Herot. As they are sleeping, Grendel's mother attacks in retaliation for the murder of her son. She carries off her son's body parts and takes Esher, Hrothgar's close friend and trusted advisor. The Geats follow but cannot save Esher. Beowulf dons his woven mail shirt for protection and plunges into the monster-filled lake to pursue his quarry. Hrothgar's courtier, Unferth, who earlier taunted Beowulf about his triumphs, now lends Beowulf his sword, Hrunting, although the sword turns out to be useless against the monster's skin.

As he tires during the fight and it seems Grendel's mother will win, Beowulf spies a gigantic sword on the wall of the battlehall to which she's dragged him. It is this sword, blessed with the magic of the giants who made it, which he uses to slay her by cutting through her neck. Beowulf brings the monster's head and the hilt of the giants' sword to Hrothgar. Another feast is held and the Geats are sent home with even more gifts from the joyful Hrothgar. Unferth makes a gift of Hrunting to Beowulf.

Once home, Beowulf recounts his adventures for his lord, Higlac, and gives him the gifts Hrothgar sent. Higlac, in turn, rewards Beowulf with the golden sword which had belonged to his father and Beowulf's grandfather, in addition to giving him land and houses. After the deaths of both Higlac and his son, Herdred, the crown falls to Beowulf. Fifty years into his rule, yet a third monster appears—this time in Geatland.

This dragon is awakened by a slave who accidentally discovers the hidden path into his tower. Seeing the dragon, the slave grabs one of the treasures surrounding him and flees for his life. The dragon, angry at being aroused and robbed, waits until nightfall; then, he uses his own fire and smoke to burn down the houses of the Geats as they watch in horror.

Beowulf orders an iron shield be made for him, since a wooden one would be no protection against the fire, and proceeds to face his own death by battling the dragon, but fully intending to take the dragon's life as well. He plans to fight alone, rather than risk the lives of others, although a dozen soldiers accompany him to the dragon's tower. It is the slave who leads them to the proper place. Weaponless and angry, Beowulf seeks the dragon, and a fiery battle ensues with the dragon seemingly the victor. However, after all his soldiers but Wiglaf flee, Wiglaf urges Beowulf on to victory and helps to kill the dragon by stabbing him with a dagger.

During the battle, Beowulf is badly burned and fatally wounded in the neck. Before his funeral pyre is built, his soldiers march past his body, having to pass the 50-foot corpse of the dragon first. The dragon's corpse is tossed into the sea and Beowulf is given the funeral he requested: burned along with his helmets, battle shields, and mail shirts. Finally, ten days are spent building a tall tower at the water's edge in which to house his ashes. Upon its completion, 12 of the bravest Geats ride around it on horseback telling stories of Beowulf's bravery and victories, weeping as they do so.

Estimated Reading Time

While this poem is only 3,182 lines, it is full of visual imagery and complicated family lineage; therefore, it is suggested the poem be read in three parts: the first dealing with Grendel and ending at line 1,250; the second dealing with Grendel's mother and ending at line 2,220; and the third dealing with the dragon, which comprises the remainder of the poem. One hour for each of the three sections, totaling three hours, should be more than sufficient for reading *Beowulf*. Since different editions of the poem will have various line numbers and spelling of the names, it is important to know which was used in writing this study guide. It is: Raffel, Burton. *Beowulf: A New Translation*. New York: The New American Library, 1963.

SECTION TWO

Part I

Lines 1–370

New Characters:

Beowulf: *the protagonist of the poem*

Hrothgar: *the Danish king who requests Beowulf's help in slaying the monster, Grendel*

Grendel: *the monster who has kept Hrothgar in misery for 12 years*

Wulfgar: *born Swedish, now the Danish king Hrothgar's herald*

Summary

The poem opens with a genealogy of the ruling Danes beginning with Shild, moving to his son Beo, then to Beo's son Healfdane, and on to Healfdane's three sons—Hergar, Hrothgar, and Halga the Good—and his daughter, Yrs. Hrothgar's building of Herot for his armies, as the ruling Danish king, is explained. The monster, Grendel, annoyed by the noise of the building and then the soldiers living in Herot, was awakened. He arrived when the soldiers were sleeping and attacked, killing 30 of them. There were tears and laments, but he attacked the next night as well. The soldiers realized they must stay away from Herot in order to be safe and did so for 12 years, much to Hrothgar's grief.

Beowulf, in Geatland, hears of this and vows to kill Grendel. He outfits his boats and sails with a band of 14 of his bravest soldiers. Once landing upon the Danish shore, they are challenged

by the sentry who eventually leads them to Herot himself, after hearing Beowulf's explanation of how they have come to kill Grendel. There, Hrothgar's herald (Wulfgar) asks who they are. Beowulf responds that he must speak to Hrothgar to give him the answer to that question. Wulfgar rushes to his king to urge him to receive Beowulf and his men.

Analysis

The poem is set approximately 200 years before its performances. People were impressed with stories of kings and wars in their history, fictional or factual. The genealogy is apparently for the purpose of "setting the stage" and establishing Hrothgar's credentials. It also establishes Beowulf's bravery in coming to kill the monster with a band of only 14 men and making the voyage without trepidation. Grendel's inherent perniciousness is implied by the explanation that he is descended from Cain, a fallen Biblical character. The stage is now set for a poem worth staying to hear, with royalty, warriors, and at least one battle between good and evil.

Study Questions

1. Why is Hrothgar's lineage given?
2. Why is Grendel's lineage given?
3. What is Herot?
4. Why did Hrothgar build Herot?
5. Why did Herot lay empty for 12 years?
6. Why did Grendel attack Herot?
7. Why hasn't Hrothgar rid Herot of Grendel?
8. Why does Beowulf come to Denmark?
9. Why does the sentry personally lead Beowulf and his men to Herot after hearing their reason for coming to Denmark?
10. Why does Wulfgar, the herald, urge Hrothgar to see Beowulf?

Answers

1. Hrothgar's lineage is given to establish that he is a king. It also serves to ready the audience for the kind of poem it enjoys—one dealing with royalty, myths, or history.

2. Grendel's lineage is given because the audience of the poem belongs to a culture shifting from paganism to Christianity. While the monster is a pagan symbol, he is descended from Cain—a fallen Biblical character—and lives "down in the darkness," a metaphor for Hell. He is a bridge between paganism and Christianity and also holds out the promise of a battle between good and evil in the poem.

3. Herot is the sumptuously-built meadhall ordered by the Danish king, Hrothgar. It is a beautiful, huge, towering place with hammered gold gables.

4. Hrothgar ordered Herot built as a meadhall for his brave warriors in which they would live, hold their feasts, and receive their rewards from him.

5. Herot has lain empty for the past 12 years because the first night the Danish soldiers slept there Grendel attacked, killing 30 of them. The attacks continued until the soldiers realized the only way to avoid dying at Grendel's will was to avoid Herot.

6. Grendel was awakened by the noise and commotion caused by the building of Herot. Then he was annoyed by the noise of the soldiers living and feasting there. His initial attack was caused by these factors. Thereafter, he simply liked how easy it was to kill the soldiers as they slept.

7. Since the soldiers quickly realized the only way to avoid being killed by Grendel was to avoid Herot, Hrothgar had no soldiers willing to go there. Without the soldiers, he had no way of ridding Herot of Grendel.

8. The tale of Grendel's victory and Hrothgar's misery spread, even across the sea to Geatland. Beowulf, feeling he is a brave and skilled soldier, brings a band of 14 of the bravest Geat warriors to kill Grendel for Hrothgar and rid Herot of its emptiness and misery.

9. The sentry is impressed by Beowulf's openly approaching the Danish shore and the weapons the Geats carry. Once Beowulf says they have come to kill Grendel, the sentry cannot be helpful enough, even if it means personally taking them to Herot, weapons and all.

10. Wulfgar, the herald, urges Hrothgar to see Beowulf because the band's weapons and armor suggest they are a prosperous lot; Beowulf is a mighty warrior, possibly one who could rid them of Grendel.

Suggested Essay Topics

1. Discuss how the importance of lineage, as seen in *Beowulf*, has changed in modern culture. Cite specific examples of cases where lineage is still discussed and considered important today—i.e., the few remaining royal families, members of families with long histories of political involvement, and children of notorious or celebrated people. Also note ways in which lineage has, and unfortunately, continues to be used against people in modern culture.

2. Beowulf comes to the Danes to assist Hrothgar's men in the defeat of Grendel. Yet it has been 12 years since Grendel's last attack on Herot. Discuss what might have happened during these 12 years to keep Grendel's need for vengeance alive, and why a young leader brought 14 men across the sea to assist in the battle.

Lines 371–835

New Characters:

Edgetho: *Beowulf's father, the link between Hrothgar and Beowulf*

Higlac: *Beowulf's uncle and lord*

Unferth: *Hrothgar's courtier who taunts Beowulf about the stories of his bravery*

Brecca: *a childhood companion of Beowulf's*

Welthow: *Hrothgar's wife*

Summary

Hrothgar remembers Edgetho's son, Beowulf, and eagerly sends Wulfgar to fetch him. Beowulf boasts of his previous conquests and promises Hrothgar that he will kill Grendel. While the Danish king is pleased that Beowulf has come in friendship, he also thinks it is in repayment for his having averted a war by ending the feud Edgetho began with the Wulfings (another tribe) years ago. After further explaining the situation with Grendel, Hrothgar orders a feast for the Geats.

At the feast, Unferth taunts Beowulf with the stories he's heard of Beowulf's youthful swimming contest with his companion, Brecca. Beowulf responds with his own version of this story. Welthow is attentive to Beowulf and, pleased with his boasts, reports to her king that he is sincere.

Later, as the Geats sleep, Grendel attacks and kills a young warrior, Hondshew. Beowulf does battle with the monster, pulling off his claw, arm, and shoulder using his bare hands, as he had vowed he would. This method of counter-attack becomes a necessity when the Geats realize their weapons are useless—they have been bewitched into harmlessness by the monster himself. Grendel escapes to his lair, only to die of his wounds. His claw, arm, and shoulder are hung from the rafters at Herot.

Analysis

Although Beowulf is seemingly overconfident and boastful, he does have a history of killing the beasts he says he will. He is duti-

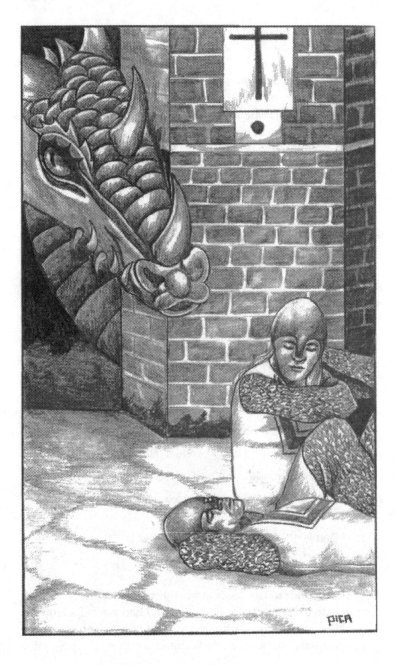

ful to his lord, Higlac, and seems respectful despite the boasting.
While Unferth plays the "devil's advocate" in taunting Beowulf,
Beowulf believes his own version of the youthful contest and turns
it into another occasion for telling of his glorious feats, rather than
belligerently arguing with the doubting Unferth.

Welthow listens carefully to the boasting and decides for her-
self that this brash, young man has a right to his boasts; or, is this
just a desperate hope on her part that he will succeed in killing
Grendel? Hrothgar also seems desperate while, at the same time,
acknowledging the veracity of Beowulf's life, if not his boasts.
Beowulf is brave and conscientious, not just a braggart, as he shows
when he stays awake while the other soldiers sleep in Herot after
the feast. His bravery and sense of ethics seem to equal his desire
for glory.

Study Questions

1. How does Hrothgar know of Beowulf?

2. What information does Beowulf's greeting to Hrothgar include?

3. What are the activities at the feast?

4. How does Unferth taunt Beowulf?

5. What is Beowulf's response to Unferth's taunts?

6. How does Welthow react to Beowulf?

7. Why does Beowulf meet Grendel bare-handed?

8. How may Grendel's attack be described?

9. Why are the Geats' weapons useless when they rush to Beowulf's aid?

10. What is done with the prize of the battle?

Answers

1. Years prior to Grendel's attacks, Beowulf's father, Edgetho,
   came to Hrothgar for help. Edgetho had started a feud by
   killing a Wulfing warrior, Hathlaf; the conflict threatened to
   become a war between the Wulfings and the Geats. Edgetho's

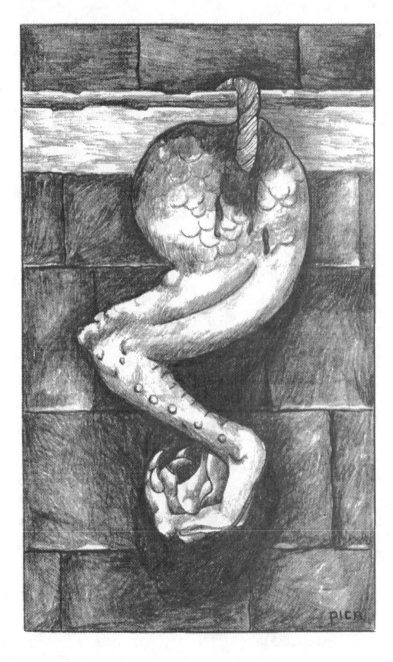

own people refused him until the feud was settled. The newly crowned, young Danish king Hrothgar was able to end the feud by sending treasure to the Wulfings, and by convincing Edgetho to swear he would keep the peace, thereby averting war. Beowulf was a young child at this time.

2. Beowulf's greeting to Hrothgar includes the following information: Higlac is his lord and relation; he (Beowulf) is a soldier of some renown (he elucidates his fame with several anecdotes); he wants to kill Grendel with only his bare hands and possibly the help of his soldiers, exclusively; and he explains what should be done with his possessions should he be killed by Grendel.

3. At the feast, the Danes surrender their seats to the Geats and serve them mead (a drink made of water, honey, malt, and yeast which is fermented). Poets sing as the Danes and Geats eat and drink.

4. Unferth taunts Beowulf at the feast by calling him a "boastful fool" and recounting the tale of his swimming contest with Brecca in such a way that it makes Beowulf seem a headstrong, irresponsible boy with no regard for the advice of his elders. He also says that Beowulf lost this contest, as he will the upcoming one with Grendel.

5. Beowulf's response to Unferth's taunts is that Unferth is drunk and has confused the facts. Beowulf proceeds to tell him that he was actually the winner of the swimming match, and that he achieved this victory by swimming through a frozen sea and battling nine sea-monsters. He continues by vilifying Unferth as someone who has won no battles and murdered his own brother. In concluding, he reaffirms his vow to kill Grendel.

6. Welthow serves Beowulf the mead after first serving her husband and his soldiers. She thinks of him as God's answer to their prayers of ridding themselves of Grendel. She is so pleased with his determination to kill Grendel, or be killed himself, that she returns to Hrothgar's side to repeat this to her husband.

7.   Beowulf fights Grendel with his bare hands because he be-
     lieves Grendel is neither stronger nor braver than he. He
     thinks his shield and sword would make Grendel helpless,
     which would be unfair if this is an even match in strength
     and bravery. Beowulf expects God to choose the victor un-
     less Grendel dies of fright first upon seeing a soldier brave
     enough to face him weaponless.

8.   Grendel hurriedly and silently slides straight to Herot where
     he snaps open the door, tearing off its hinges. He stops for a
     moment as he spies the sleeping warriors to delight in what
     he sees as his upcoming feast. He grabs Hondshew, rips him
     apart, drinks his blood, and eats him. Next, he clutches
     Beowulf, who instantly grabs Grendel's claws. Realizing this
     is not a Dane he can kill quickly as usual, Grendel struggles
     to flee from this Geat. Herot trembles as the two sweep down
     its aisles. Screams ring out as they grapple. Beowulf's sol-
     diers jump into the fray, only to find their weapons useless.
     Grendel, growing weaker and angrier, twists away in pain,
     leaving his claw, arm, and shoulder with Beowulf as he flees
     to his den.

9.   The Geats' weapons are useless because Grendel had laid
     spells on them, rendering them blunt.

10. The prizes of battle—Grendel's claw, arm, and shoulder—
     are hung from the rafters of Herot.

Suggested Essay Topics

1.   Despite the fact that Beowulf is a boastful and confident
     young man, he has a history of keeping his promises. Dis-
     cuss how this is evidenced in this section of the poem.

2.   When Beowulf first arrives at Herot, Unferth tells the story
     of Beowulf's swimming contest with Brecca; then Beowulf
     gives his version of the same contest. How do you account
     for each of the differences in Unferth and Beowulf's versions
     of this contest?

Lines 836–1,250

New Characters:

Siegmund: *the protagonist of a poem sung at the feast to urge "good character" in obtaining glory as opposed to Hermod, who demonstrated "bad character" in the same pursuit*

Finn: *also sung about in poetry to demonstrate "bad character" since he attacked his wife's people without warning, killing her son and brother. He then forced his enemies into a peace treaty and was, eventually, murdered by them.*

Hermod: *a previous Danish king whose character was as poor as his military skill was great*

Hrothulf: *Hrothgar's nephew who was raised by Hrothgar and Welthow after his own father died when he was a young boy*

Summary

The next morning, crowds joyfully arrive to view the scene of the battle and Grendel's dying path back to his den. Horse races are held and Beowulf's praises are sung. Hrothgar, upon seeing Grendel's claw, arm, and shoulder hanging from the rafters of Herot, offers Beowulf any reward he may desire, whereupon Beowulf apologizes for not having Grendel's corpse to present to the Danish king. Unferth abandons any thought of taunting Beowulf and another feast is ordered by Hrothgar in celebration of the rebirth of Herot, which will once again be the home of the Danish warriors.

At the feast, Beowulf is presented with prizes by the grateful Hrothgar: a golden banner, a helmet, a coat of mail, an ancient sword, and eight horses with golden bridles—one wearing the jeweled saddle shaped like a war-seat which had carried Hrothgar to war. Toasts are offered and the other Geats are also rewarded. Gold is given as compensation for Hondshew's life. Songs, laughter, and poetry ring in Herot. Welthow joins Beowulf as he sits between her two sons while being given even more gifts—jewels, this time—and tells him of her faith in him. The feast ends and the Danish soldiers prepare for sleep in Herot with their weapons at their heads and hands and their mail shirts on their chests.

Analysis

Although the beast, Grendel, is dead, there seems to be an overabundance of joy which rings false. The queen is saying that there are no plots, no whispers in Herot that night and that she has faith in both Hrothgar and Beowulf; but, then again, it seems unnecessary to reaffirm her faith in the king and the savior of her land. Perhaps Welthow is trying too hard to present the image of a united, untroubled people.

At the feast, poetry is sung not only of Siegmund, a positive example, but also of Finn, who was supposed to be quite the opposite. Could this be foreshadowing that all is not well in Denmark? It would be simplistic to assume that any upcoming problem would be in the political area; the foreshadowing seems to deal more with the character one exhibits in his quest for glory, since the protagonist of each poem was involved in just such a quest. Perhaps this is a warning to Beowulf that it is not yet time to rest.

Study Questions

1. Why do the crowds come to Herot?

2. What is the song of Siegmund?

3. Who is Hermod?

4. How does Hrothgar express his gratitude to Beowulf?

5. How does Beowulf describe the battle with Grendel when speaking to Hrothgar?

6. What is the song of Finn?

7. What is it Welthow tells Hrothgar when the songs are finished?

8. What does she say to Beowulf?

9. What is to happen to Herot once this feast is over?

10. What are the soldiers' sleeping arrangements?

Answers

1. The crowds come to Herot in order to trace Grendel's path from Herot to the edge of the lake in which he had his den.

The water is still bloody and swirling, which delights the crowds since this confirms his death.

2. The song of Siegmund is about another dragon slayer who earns glory by single-handedly pinning a dragon to the wall of its own lair. The dragon dissolves in its own blood and Siegmund is rewarded with treasures and fame.

3. Hermod, as we are told in lines 899–911, is born a king, but "pride and defeat and betrayal" are his lot after he continuously ignores his people's wishes and wise men's warnings. He rules by his own vanity, which leads to misery for all and, ultimately, his death.

4. Hrothgar commands that Herot be cleansed and another feast be held, at which Beowulf is toasted, the object of the new poems being created, praised by Welthow and Hrothgar, and given even more gifts: a coat of mail, a helmet, a golden banner, an ancient sword, eight golden bridled horses (one bearing the jeweled saddle Hrothgar had used for war), golden armbands, a beautiful necklace, and other jewels.

5. Beowulf tells Hrothgar how he tried to kill Grendel by ripping his claw off, but that Grendel fled from him, leaving his claw, arm, and shoulder behind. He says Grendel ran in fear and that he, Beowulf, wishes he had the monster's body in Herot to show to Hrothgar.

6. The song of Finn relates how Finn attacked his wife's people with no warning, killing her brother (the king of Denmark) and son in the battle. Finn's troops were half decimated, so he forced the Danes into a peace treaty which provided each group with half the kingdoms. Because he killed Hnaf, their king, they secretly swore revenge—which they achieved by murdering him after a year of living with Finn in his land. This led to the destruction of all Finn's land and possessions and the kidnapping of his queen.

7. Welthow tells Hrothgar to be a generous king and to be grateful to Beowulf. She assures him that his nephew, Hrothulf, will protect their sons, Hrethric and Hrothmund, when death finally takes him, just as Hrothgar and Welthow had pro-

tected and given a home to Hrothulf when his father died.

8. Welthow tells Beowulf to enjoy his gifts and to let his fame and strength grow. She implores him to think kindly of her sons and extend his protection to them. She is emphatic about there being peace and loyalty in Herot.

9. Once the feast is over, Herot is to revert to its original purpose: to be the meadhall and living quarters of Hrothgar's troops.

10. The soldiers sleep with their shields at the ends of their pillows, helmets near their heads, spears near their hands, and wearing their mail shirts while laying on blankets and pillows spread on the floor which the benches for the feast had occupied.

Suggested Essay Topics

1. At the second feast, poetry is sung; each poem seems to have a specific moral for the listeners, rather than just entertainment. What are the lessons inherent in the songs of Siegmund and Finn?

2. Hrothgar, an older king, relies upon Beowulf, a young warrior, to save his country. While Hrothgar is considered a good and fair king, Beowulf is something of a legend already. How does the poem indicate, specifically, that each respects the other's accomplishments?

SECTION THREE

Part II

Lines 1,251–1,650

New Character:

Esher: *Hrothgar's close friend and advisor, killed by Grendel's mother*

Summary

Grendel's mother, wanting revenge for her son's murder, attacks the Danes as they sleep in Herot for the first time in 12 years. Awakened, the soldiers grab their swords as she takes Esher and flees for her life. Shouts erupt from Herot when the soldiers realize Grendel's mother absconded with her son's claw, as well. Hrothgar sends for Beowulf, who was sleeping elsewhere in more comfort with his own men. When they reach Hrothgar, the sorrowful king explains what has happened and asks Beowulf to once again slay the monster who threatens his people.

Once Beowulf agrees, Hrothgar leads his soldiers in following the monster's tracks through the forest to the rocky hills and slippery cliffs, and then to a lake with bloody, bubbling water. The Danes see Esher's bloody head on the cliff above the lake and sound their battle horns, scaring away the snakes, serpents, and sea beasts who live in the lake. Beowulf wounds one of these creatures, which is fished out of the lake to be examined by all. He dons his woven mail armor, knowing he will need it to protect himself from the monster's claws. Unferth then lends Hrunting, his sword, to Beowulf.

Ready, Beowulf gives Hrothgar instructions as to the disposi-
tion of his possessions should he die; he then leaps into the lake.
His descent is lengthy and terminates in Grendel's mother's arms.

Seeing she cannot harm him through the armor he wears, she
carries him to her lair which is actually a battlehall. While he is
unable to free his sword, other creatures come to investigate and
stay to attempt attacking him through his shirt of woven mail. The
roof of the battlehall protects Beowulf from both the heat of the
water and the other creatures. Beowulf attacks with Hrunting, but
to no avail; nor is his helmet effective in protecting him from
Grendel's mother.

He attempts to fight the she monster barehanded in his fury
at the thought of losing fame because his weapons and helmet are
ineffective. As he grows tired, his opponent overthrows him and
sits on his stomach while she draws a dagger. Again, his armor saves
him.

He spies a magical sword made by giants hanging on the wall
of the battlehall and uses it to kill Grendel's mother via a slice to
the neck which breaks the bones therein. A brilliant light begins to
shine and Beowulf uses it to hunt for Grendel. He finds the
monster's corpse and beheads it.

The Danish soldiers and their king have already left after
spending most of the day staring into the lake and discussing
Beowulf's almost certain death. Steadfast, the Geats remain as the
sword melts, the treasures in the lair are uncovered, and Beowulf
returns through the now clear waters of the lake with Grendel's
head and the unmelted hilt of the jeweled giants' sword. The Geats
carry Beowulf's armor and helmet, as they do Grendel's head
(which he wants to bring to Hrothgar) while the lake's water becomes thick with the blood of Grendel's mother. Upon reaching
Herot, Beowulf carries the head by its hair directly to Hrothgar
where he and his queen sit drinking.

Analysis

Hrothgar, in his grief at the appearance of another monster
and the killing of his close friend and advisor, Esher, seems to de-
spair at Grendel's mother's appearance, perhaps thinking this por-
tends another 12 years of silence in Herot. Rather than test his

soldiers' weapons to ascertain if they are as useless against the mother as they were against the son, he simply assumes they are—even though it is the now-dead son who bewitched them. By immediately sending for Beowulf, and then by losing faith in Beowulf's potential for victory over Grendel's mother so quickly, it seems as if Hrothgar has given up all hope of protecting his people and his land.

Beowulf, for his part, is only too happy to tend to Grendel's mother in the hopes of achieving more fame. He offers no excuses when Hrothgar asks for his intervention and, in his response to the Danish king's appeal, notes "...fame after death is the noblest of all goals." True to his feeling, when Hrunting and his helmet are ineffective against Grendel's mother, he becomes angry at the thought of being robbed of the glory of killing another monster and fights her barehanded, as he had her son. It seems Beowulf remembers the lessons he's learned from the past too well, while Hrothgar forgets his too soon and too easily.

Study Questions

1. What happens the first night the Danes return to sleep in Herot?

2. Why does Grendel's mother flee from Herot?

3. Why does Hrothgar send for Beowulf?

4. How does Beowulf respond to Hrothgar's request?

5. Where does Hrothgar lead Beowulf?

6. How may the lake containing Grendel's mother and her lair be described?

7. Why is Beowulf careful to wear his armor?

8. How does Unferth's behavior toward Beowulf change now?

9. How does Beowulf attempt to save his life when he realizes his weapons and helmet are ineffective?

10. What are Hrothgar and his soldiers doing while Beowulf battles Grendel's mother?

Answers

1. The first night the Danes sleep in Herot after 12 years of avoiding the hall because of Grendel's attacks, his mother— seeking revenge for the murder of her son—mounts her own attack.

2. Grendel's mother flees Herot since she is vastly outnumbered by the Danish soldiers, who are not only using their shields to protect themselves against her attack, but their swords in a counter-attack upon her. She realizes she cannot win this battle and runs for her life, taking Esher and Grendel's claw with her.

3. Hrothgar sends for Beowulf to ask him to, once again, rid Herot of the monster—in this case, Grendel's mother.

4. Beowulf tells Hrothgar that revenge is better than mourning forever and that fame after death is to be sought before he vows to kill this monster, too.

5. Hrothgar leads Beowulf through the forest, hills, and cliffs in following Grendel's mother's tracks to the bloody, bubbling lake in which she has her lair.

6. The lake containing Grendel's mother's lair may be described as horrifying. Not only is the water bloody and bubbling, but it is hot, swirling, and filled with snakes, serpents, and sea beasts. To add to the horror, Esher's bloody head can be seen on the cliff above the lake.

7. Beowulf is careful to wear his armor because he knows the hammered links of the woven mail will protect his heart from monster claws. He wears the helmet to protect him from sword blows.

8. Upon Beowulf's arrival at Herot, Unferth drunkenly taunts him with the story of a childhood swimming meet with Brecca, saying it was foolhardy and Beowulf egotistical. Now that Beowulf has killed Grendel barehanded and is on the brink of attempting to kill Grendel's mother, Unferth has obviously revised his opinion of Beowulf since he lends him his most prized possession—his ancient sword, Hrunting.

9. Even though Beowulf's weapons and helmet prove ineffective, he is able to save his life by tossing them aside and fighting Grendel's mother both barehanded and bareheaded. His mail shirt does deflect the blows when Grendel's mother tries to stab him. There is a magical sword, made by giants, hanging on the wall of the battlehall. Beowulf uses that to slice her at the neck, killing her.

10. While Beowulf battles with Grendel's mother, Hrothgar and his soldiers are staring into the lake, watching it surge and spurt blood as they talk of the Geat warrior. They agree that Grendel's mother must be the victor in this battle, but wait anyway. Later in the day, the Danes and their king leave while the Geats remain, awaiting the hopefully triumphant arrival of their leader from the depths of the horrifying lake.

Suggested Essay Topics

1. Discuss the specifics of how and why Unferth's opinion of Beowulf changes after his defeat of Grendel and Grendel's mother, and Unferth's loan of a sword to Beowulf.

2. Explain how Grendel's mother's actions are both similar and dissimilar to those of a grieving human mother, had her child been murdered.

Lines 1,651–1,887

New Character:

Hrethric: *Hrothgar's eldest son*

Summary

Beowulf gives Hrothgar Grendel's head and the hilt of the jeweled, magical sword made by the giants. As he does so, he recounts the battle with Grendel's mother and promises that Herot will be safe henceforth. Examining the sword hilt, Hrothgar discovers the story of its giant-makers. It explains how they suffered a war between good and evil and were then swept away by floods. He finds the name of the owner in Runic letters on the hilt.

Hrothgar then advises Beowulf how to be a good prince, warning him not to be like Hermod, who allowed his poor character to make him an unjust and disliked ruler. Beowulf is cautioned to remember his mortality and shun pride as a ruling emotion. Yet another feast is held to celebrate the second monster's demise and is enjoyed by Geats and Danes alike.

The following morning, before the Geats begin their sea voyage home, Unferth arrives to present Beowulf with Hrunting, not as a loan this time, but as a gift. In his farewell to Hrothgar, Beowulf thanks him for being a gracious host and offers his services (and those of his lord) at any time they may be needed; he also reassures Hrothgar that Hrethric is more than welcome to visit.

Hrothgar praises Beowulf, telling him what a good king he will be when he is eventually offered the throne of Geatland and showers him with more gifts. Knowing he is too old to have the opportunity to see Beowulf again, Hrothgar begins crying as he kisses him farewell and the Geats leave.

Analysis

Hrothgar, while delighted with Beowulf both as a person and as the victor in the two battles with the monsters, seems to understand how pride can undermine a person's character, as he

demonstrates by telling the story of Hermod. He seems to care greatly for Beowulf and worry about him; he knows the young Geat will become a great king sometime in the future, and tries to advise him as to the best way to do it. He obviously regards Beowulf with great affection and is sad that they will never see each other again, since he is old and the distance between them will be vast now that the Geat is returning home.

The young Geat seems so satisfied at obtaining glory by killing Grendel and his mother that he does not hear this advice. Perhaps it is his youth that prevents him from thinking about his mortality as Hrothgar urges. He makes no comment on the story of Hermod after it is told, instead declaring that he is certain his lord, Higlac, will support him in returning should Hrothgar have any more troubles.

Study Questions

1. What is the sign of victory Beowulf gives to Hrothgar?

2. How does Beowulf feel his life was saved?

3. What does Hrothgar do when Beowulf gives him the sword hilt?

4. What happened to the magical giants who made the sword?

5. What is the story of Hermod?

6. What, specifically, is Hrothgar warning Beowulf about in telling this story?

7. What is the occasion for Unferth's visit?

8. What promises does Beowulf make as he takes his leave of Hrothgar?

9. Hrothgar says he is pleased with Beowulf for what reasons?

10. Why does Hrothgar weep?

Answers

1. The sign of victory that Beowulf gives to Hrothgar is Grendel's head. When he won the earlier battle with Grendel, the monster was able to escape, minus his claw, arm, and shoulder,

to die in his lair. At that time, Beowulf apologized to Hrothgar for not being able to bring him the monster's body. After slaying Grendel's mother, he finds the body in the lair that the mother and son shared and beheads it, bringing this prize to the Danish king.

2. Beowulf explains that God showed him the giants' magical sword which he used to slay Grendel's mother after Hrunting proved to be ineffective. (Remember, this is an English poem about the Danes and Geats written at the time when Christianity was first gaining acceptance.)

3. When Beowulf gives Hrothgar the sword hilt, he examines it minutely, finding the story of the giants' demise and the name of the owner written in the Runic language.

4. According to the story written on the jeweled sword hilt, the giants survived a battle between good and evil only to be swept away as a people during a flood created by God, whom they hated.

5. Hermod's story tells of a former Danish king who was very strong, but had mad rages during which he killed his own people. He was insensitive to his people's needs and ended his life without followers, a lonely man. He shared none of his wealth nor his glory with his soldiers.

6. Hrothgar is warning Beowulf to remember his own mortality; while all may be well now, it may not always be so. In addition, he fears Beowulf will allow his pride to interfere with the way he rules when he becomes the Geat king, as Hrothgar feels he eventually will.

7. Unferth completely revises his opinion of Beowulf when the Geat enters the lake to kill Grendel's mother alone, since all others were afraid to do so. He wants him to have Hrunting as a gift given in admiration of Beowulf's fearlessness and strength.

8. When Beowulf takes his leave of Hrothgar, he promises to come immediately with a battalion of 1,000 soldiers supplied by Higlac should Hrothgar summon him or if he hears of a

need on Hrothgar's part. He also promises that Hrethric will be made very welcome in Geatland should he visit.

9. Hrothgar says he is pleased with Beowulf because of his strength and his wisdom. He is also pleased because he feels Beowulf will one day be a great king in his own land, providing he remembers his mortality and does not allow his pride to rule him.

10. Hrothgar weeps because he knows he will never again see this young man he has grown to love and who has done so much for his people. Hrothgar is an old man at this point and Beowulf is sailing home, a great distance.

Suggested Essay Topics

1. Discuss the lesson of Hermod's story, and the "message" his death would give the audience.

2. Although Hrunting was useless in Beowulf's attack on Grendel's mother and this almost costs his life, Unferth gives the ancient sword to the Geat as a gift before he sails for home. Why do you think he does this?

3. How do you account for Hrothgar's regarding Beowulf as a son when he already has two of his own in addition to a son-in-law?

4. Why do you think Beowulf goes through the trouble of bringing Grendel's head to Hrothgar after he'd already apologized for not having it at the time he killed Grendel and Hrothgar seemingly acccepted the lack of a corpse?

Lines 1,888–2,220

New Characters:

Higd: *Higlac's wife*

Thrith: *Offa's wife who, prior to her marriage, wantonly bore false witness, causing the unnecessary deaths of whomever she chose to accuse*

Freaw: *the daughter Hrothgar married to Ingeld in the futile hope of settling the feud between his people and his son-in-law's*

Summary

As Beowulf and his men go to their ship, the Danish sentry rides to meet them—not to challenge them, but to tell them how welcome they will be at home. Beowulf gives the ship's watchman a sword hammered in gold and the Geats load their vessel with the horses, armor, and treasures. They set sail. The waiting Geats run to greet them when they arrive home and carry their prizes to Higlac. The band of Geats who are returning from Denmark hasten to greet Higlac.

Higlac seats Beowulf next to him and mead is served. Higlac is happy to see his nephew again, saying he feared he would never see him again. Beowulf tells his lord of his battles with the two monsters, the three feasts, and the impending marriage of Freaw to Ingeld in what Beowulf feels is a futile attempt by Hrothgar to end the feud between their peoples. In presenting the banner, helmet, armor, and sword given to him by Hrothgar for Higlac, Beowulf explains their heritage as Hrothgar had asked him to do. Then the four horses are brought in and presented to Higlac. Higd is given the necklace sent to her by Welthow, Hrothgar's queen, and three other horses. Higlac bestows the sword of his father and Beowulf's grandfather upon the young Geatish prince, in addition to bestowing him with land and houses.

Having refused the throne once before, Beowulf accepts it after the deaths of both Higlac and his son, Herdred. He rules for 50 years and is an old man when a dragon is awakened by a thief stealing one of its treasures. The beast arises to terrorize Geatland.

Analysis

It seems that Beowulf was well-raised by his lord's father, Hrethel. Not only does he do exactly as Hrothgar instructed in presenting all his gifts to Higlac, but he also explains their heritage as the older Danish king had requested. Welthow's gifts to Higd are given with the same promptness and courtesy. It must be pointed out that princes and warriors often kept the gifts bestowed upon them as prizes, instead of giving these gifts to their kings.

Hrothgar cautioned Beowulf against letting pride be his ruling emotion; between the respect and loyalty he shows for his sovereigns and the kindness (as in presenting the man who watched the boat with a sword for his troubles) and deference he shows to his elders, the reader begins to wonder if perhaps Beowulf has taken Hrothgar's stories and admonitions to heart. When he is urged to ascend the Geatish throne upon Higlac's death, he does not, preferring to stand aside so that Herdred, Higlac's son, could have that honor and responsibility. Only when Herdred also dies does Beowulf agree to take the throne.

It appears that, while amassing all the glory and fame he could, Beowulf is simultaneously learning the ethics necessary to be a proper king. The poems sung at the feasts and the stories told to him by the Danish king do not miss their mark. It is noted that he was noble (although thought lazy) while still a boy; it is obvious that all his fame and glory did not destroy this nobility.

Study Questions

1. What does Beowulf give the boat watcher?
2. How are the Geats greeted once they arrive home?
3. What is the story of Thrith?
4. Why didn't Higlac initially allow Beowulf to go to Hrothgar's aid when they first heard of the monsters threatening Herot?
5. What is Beowulf's opinion of Hrothgar's plan concerning Ingeld and Freaw?
6. What is the heritage of the gifts Beowulf gives Higlac from Hrothgar?

7. What gift does Higlac bestow upon Beowulf?

8. At what point in the family lineage does Beowulf agree to assume the throne of Geatland?

9. How long does Beowulf rule peacefully?

10. What breaks the peace during Beowulf's kingship?

Answers

1. Beowulf gives the man who watched their boat a sword with hammered gold wound around its handle as a reward for staying behind during their battles and to honor him for this sacrifice.

2. Upon arriving home, the Geats are greeted by joyous harbor guards who have been waiting and watching for their arrival for days. It is they who anchor and moor the boat, then carry the treasures it holds to Higlac's home.

3. Thrith is a princess who used her vicious tongue to accuse people she disliked of wrong-doing, which led to their arrest and, then, death. Her marriage to Offa eventually ended this injustice.

4. Higlac fears for his nephew, Beowulf, when first he hears of the monsters in Denmark, and prevents him from going to fight them. The stories of Hrothgar's misery move him but he allows the Danes to fight their own battle until it is clear Beowulf is needed. Even at this point, he thinks he might never again behold his nephew once he does depart.

5. Beowulf thinks Hrothgar's plan to marry his daughter, Freaw, to Ingeld in order to end the feud between the two peoples is a poor one. He is not opposed to Freaw marrying an older man, but fears that Ingeld's people—the Hathobards—will see the Danes wearing certain pieces of armor and remember that this armor once belonged to *their* people, which may lead a drunken Hathobard to bait a young Dane into battle due to this unexpressed bitterness. One battle is all it will take to begin a chain reaction of other battles and the war will recommence.

6. Beowulf gives Hrothgar's boarhead banner, helmet, ancient armor, and gold-carved sword to Higlac, explaining to him that they were first Hergar's—Hrothgar's older brother who held the throne until his death when Hrothgar replaced him. Hergar had refused to give them to his son, Herward, so they stayed with the throne.

7. Higlac gives Beowulf a sword worked in gold which had belonged to his father. Since Beowulf is Higlac's nephew, Higlac's father was Beowulf's grandfather. It is supposedly the best sword in Geatland.

8. Beowulf agrees to assume the throne of Geatland only when both his uncle, Higlac, and Higlac's son, Herdred—the next in line to be king after Higlac—die, although he is offered the throne upon Higlac's death.

9. Once accepting the kingship, Beowulf rules peacefully for 50 years and is considered a wise king.

10. Beowulf's peaceful rule is broken by a thief who stumbles upon a dragon's tower and steals one of his treasures, not only waking the dragon, but angering him as well.

Suggested Essay Topics

1. Beowulf follows all of Hrothgar's instructions in presenting the gifts to Higlac and Higd, including explaining the heritage of these gifts to Higlac. Not only is he courteous and correct, but his actions are also somewhat unusual since warriors often kept these gifts for themselves. Explain how and why it is possible Beowulf might be taking Hrothgar's admonitions against pride to heart.

2. Discuss the various reasons Beowulf accepts the Geatish throne only after the deaths of Higlac and Herdred. Explain why you feel this is modesty or Beowulf's genuinely enjoying the warrior life. Include why the throne was offered to Beowulf after Higlac's death, even though Herdred was next in line of succession at that time.

SECTION FOUR

Part III

Lines 2,221–2,601

New Characters:

Herdred: *Higlac and Higd's son who is next in line for the throne upon Higlac's death, although the throne is offered to—and rejected by—Beowulf at that time*

Onela: *a Swedish king married to the Danish king Healfdane's daughter, Yrs, making him Hrothgar's brother-in-law*

Herbald: *Hrethel's eldest son; killed by his younger brother, Hathcyn, in a freak hunting accident; both were Higlac's older brothers; all three brothers are raised with Beowulf as another brother (although he is actually their nephew) from the time he was a young boy*

Summary

A slave, trying to find a hiding place to avoid the master who beat him, stumbles across a dragon's lair. He steals a jeweled cup from among the treasures he finds there and flees when he realizes where he is. The treasure belongs to an ancient, lost race. The last remaining member of the race built a stone tower without doors or windows, near the sea beneath a cliff, in which to house the treasure of gold, jewels, swords, armor, and precious cups before his death. It is this tower the slave stumbles upon. After the ancient race became extinct, a flaming dragon discovered the

tower, and has been sleeping there for hundreds of years before the slave disturbs him.

The slave brings the cup to his master who is well-pleased with it. However, the dragon becomes enraged at being awakened and robbed, and tracks the slave. Having no success at finding the thief, he attacks the village, burning down the houses with his fiery breath once night arrives. He returns to his tower as daylight breaks. His people come to tell Beowulf that the dragon has burned down his hall. A miserable, guilt-ridden Beowulf immediately begins plotting the Geats' revenge.

Knowing that wood will be useless against the dragon's fiery breath, Beowulf orders an iron shield made for himself. He also knows he has not many years remaining to his life, since he has already ruled for 50 years and was not a young man when he became king. Yet, he plans to take the dragon's life as his own ends (presumably in battle with the dragon), and to do so alone. Escorted by a dozen of his men, he follows the slave, who fearfully leads the way to the tower. A weary Beowulf rests on the shore before entering the tower. He explains that he will not fight the dragon barehanded as he had done with the previous monsters because, this time, he is engaging a fire-breathing dragon and will need to protect himself long enough to kill the beast.

He strides to the entrance of the tower and becomes angry, roaring out a battle cry loud enough for the dragon within to hear. Beowulf waits at the entrance with his shield in front of him as the dragon spits fire and approaches him. Beowulf's shield holds for a while, then melts under the dragon's fire and his sword cracks as he attacks the dragon. Although Beowulf draws blood, the dragon wraps him in fire; and Beowulf knows he is dying as all his men but one run away.

Analysis

In this particular section of the poem, Beowulf summarizes his life. It seems he is not doing this so much for his people as he is for himself. He is older, has ruled for 50 years after refusing the throne when it was offered to him the first time, and is weary. Rather than seeking fame and glory, although he pays "lip service" to fame in this battle, Beowulf is being methodical and sensible. He real-

izes barehanded combat makes no sense against a fire-breathing dragon, and that he will need a shield to protect himself while battling the dragon, in order to stay alive long enough to kill the dragon. He also realizes that flammable wood will not do. While he is careful to have an iron shield fashioned for this confrontation, he does seem to be resigned that this will be his final battle. He is tired and acknowledges this to himself as he rests on the shore before facing the dragon.

He is angry, as well, as exemplified when he roars at the entrance of the tower. While this can simply be read as anger at the dragon for burning his hall and his people's homes, if it is kept in mind that Beowulf is resigned to this being the end of his life, it may also be anger at never having had a wife, a family, or an heir.

Beowulf was brought up in Hrethel's home from the time he was seven; Higlac, Hathcyn, and Herbald lived there, also. He had the opportunity to see Hrethel's grief when Hathcyn killed Herbald and may be wondering who will grieve for him as he faces his impending death. Hrethel and his sons treated Beowulf as family, but it is mentioned that Beowulf was regarded as lazy and slow at court; was this, perhaps, a young boy's attempt to prevent any relationships in a strange situation after being taken from his parents without any resistance on their part? At Hrothgar's court, while the Danish king treated him as a son, Beowulf had the comfort of knowing he would be leaving as soon as the monsters were killed and did not need to worry about any lasting relations with yet another man who wanted to treat him as a son.

Returning to his native Geatland, he refused to take the throne when Higlac was killed, insisting Herdred must be the king. Gallant, loyal, and correct as this action was, it also afforded Beowulf the opportunity to avoid having to take a queen, sire princes, and interact closely with his court members for a few more years.

He is a warrior and prefers the company of other soldiers. This fact does not necessarily suggest he is homosexual, but rather that he prefers the false intimacy of an enforced "family": his band of followers. The quests and wars are the subjects of their time together, and the membership of this family is constantly changing due to death in battle or sons joining their king's band as their fathers have done. It seems Beowulf was more comfortable avoiding

intimacy and keeping people at an emotional distance from him. Yet, while he is ready to meet his death, he appears sorry he must do so without the ties he had previously spurned.

Study Questions

1. How did the tower come to be the dragon's lair?

2. Why does the dragon burn down the Geats' homes?

3. What is Beowulf's reaction to this?

4. What does he order made for his battle with the dragon?

5. How is Herbald killed?

6. What does Beowulf say in his farewell speech to his followers?

7. How does Beowulf call the dragon?

8. How does the dragon respond to this?

9. Why does Beowulf lose the battle?

10. Where are his followers as he is losing the battle?

Answers

1. The last remaining member of an ancient race built the tower before he died to house the treasures of that now extinct race. The dragon, looking for victims, discovered the windowless, doorless tower built on the shore under a cliff and decided to use it for his lair. The dragon had slept there for hundreds of years, undisturbed.

2. A slave, seeking refuge from the master who beat him, stumbles upon the path to the tower. Once inside, he sees the dragon but manages to steal a jeweled cup before fleeing. The dragon, enraged at being awakened and robbed, attempts to track the slave. In his frustration at being unable to do so, he plans to attack at nightfall; the attack consists of burning down the people's houses and Beowulf's hall with his fiery breath.

3. Beowulf is guilt-ridden, feeling he has somehow offended God and brought his wrath upon the Geats.

4. Beowulf orders an iron shield fashioned for this battle with the fire-breathing dragon, since wood will only burn and, therefore, afford him almost no protection.

5. Hathcyn shot an arrow while hunting with his brothers but missed his mark and accidentally killed his brother, Herbald. Their father, Hrethel, was devastated by the death of his eldest son and the loss of love he felt for Hathcyn; yet, when he died, Hathcyn and Higlac, the third brother, shared the throne.

6. Beowulf tells his followers he will not fight the dragon barehanded since it is a fire-breather, but he will fight the dragon alone. He says he is the only one capable of defeating the dragon and asks that they wait for him to either win the battle or die.

7. Beowulf calls the dragon by roaring out a battle cry at the entrance to the tower. The battle cry resounds throughout the tower, assaulting the dragon's ears.

8. The dragon responds angrily, breathing fire and storming toward the entrance eager for battle.

9. Beowulf loses the battle because his iron shield melts, leaving him vulnerable to the fire breath of the dragon, and his sword cracks as he attacks, allowing him to draw blood, but not kill the dragon.

10. All of Beowulf's followers but one have run away into the forest, fearing for their lives.

Suggested Essay Topics

1. Beowulf summarizes his life as the consummate military life. Discuss how he has lived essentially alone and how, while this results in his being a wise and strong leader, it leaves him a man who must face his death realizing he has foolishly avoided having a close relationship with another human being.

2. Beowulf seems to realize this will be his final battle. Discuss the evidence for this: he summarizes his life, acknowledges his tiredness as he rests briefly before the fight, and lets out a roar of anger that seems to express his own feelings as well as lure the dragon to the fight.

3. Explain how you account for the fact that only Beowulf thinks to protect his people from the dragon when they were all horrified by the dragon's burning of their homes.

4. Using the poem itself as a reference, explain why Beowulf was compelled to fight the dragon, although this could very well mean his country would be leaderless if he were to be killed in the battle.

Lines 2,602–3,057

New Characters:

Wiglaf: *the only one of Beowulf's followers who does not flee when he fights the dragon*

Efor: *the Geat warrior who kills the Swedish king, Ongentho, and is given Higlac's daughter in marriage as a reward*

Ongentho: *the Swedish king who kills Hathcyn, the Geatish king and Hrethel's son, after Hrethel's death; killed by Higlac; Onela's father*

Summary

Wiglaf, descended from Swedes but now a Geat, is the only soldier not to flee from Beowulf's battle with the dragon. For the first time employing the armor his father, Wexstan, had taken from Onela's nephew in battle and given to him, Wiglaf rushes to Beowulf's aid, explaining that the king is now older and, despite his intention to kill this dragon alone, needs the help of younger, stronger men. He shouts encouragement to Beowulf which the dragon hears and becomes enraged by. The dragon's fire forces Wiglaf to drop his burning shield and, since his chain mail affords no protection from the heat, hide behind his king's shield with him. Beowulf uses Nagling to attempt to kill the dragon, but it falls into pieces, as all his swords do, because of his powerful thrusts. The dragon takes advantage of Beowulf's momentary helplessness and attacks, driving his tusks into Beowulf's neck.

Burning his hands in the effort, Wiglaf strikes the dragon in a lower region with his sword. As the dragon's flames begin to die, Beowulf uses his dagger to slit the beast in half. Beowulf's wound is already festering, since the dragon injected venom there when his fangs entered the old Geatish king's flesh. Beowulf collapses and Wiglaf tries to make him as comfortable as possible in these circumstances. Knowing he is dying, Beowulf asks Wiglaf to find the dragon's treasure and bring some of it to him to ease his death.

Wiglaf finds the treasure strangely illuminated by a light shining everywhere and hastens to bring some of this treasure to his

dying king. He sprinkles water on Beowulf to relieve his suffering as the old king beseeches him to become the next king. Beowulf also requests that Wiglaf build a tomb on the water's edge at the high point of that land, so sailors can see it and remember their deceased king. Having given Wiglaf his necklace, helmet, rings, and mail shirt, Beowulf dies.

Vainly endeavoring to keep Beowulf alive, Wiglaf continues to sprinkle water on the corpse as the cowardly soldiers return. He lambastes them for their reprehensible behavior and sends a messenger to tell the Geats the news of their king's death, and to warn them to beware of impending war as soon as their enemies know their king is dead. He suggests that the dragon's treasure be burned in its entirety in Beowulf's funeral pyre rather than allow anyone to enjoy it, since it was gained at the cost of their wise king's life. The soldiers file past the 50-foot corpse of the dragon and then, weeping, past Beowulf's now lifeless body.

Analysis

Beowulf's age shows as he allows Wiglaf to aid him in this final battle. Never before has he allowed another to join him in battle if he had proclaimed this would be his fight and his alone. Then again, his life is ending as he chose to live it—nearly alone, and he may be aware that this was not necessarily the best way to live it. He has an old man's perspective on what he may consider his mistakes, as well as an old man's physical limitations. He is actively sharing this battle with Wiglaf and, also, sharing his protection: the shield. This may be a willingness to share the last few moments of his life or an inclusion of Wiglaf in what Beowulf sees as the continuity of his life (as he has no heirs) since he pleads with Wiglaf, a young man to whom he has no blood ties, to become the next king.

Wiglaf has no hesitation about imperiling his life to aid his king. He had a father who took care to present him with a spear and shield, the strength of a young man, and feels a bond with Beowulf for his treatment of the family when they first emigrated from Sweden to relocate in Geatland. He does not wait for Beowulf to either ask for help nor instruct him as to what to do. He initiates the aid, inadvertently further enraging the dragon. Rather than flee at this turn of events, he confidently turns to his king to share the

shield—the actions of someone assured of cooperation in a dire situation or those of someone who has been taught to expect not to be alone.

Beowulf dies as he lived, nearly alone. He has no wife, nor heirs; the family and friends he had have predeceased him. He meets his death with only one companion, Wiglaf, a young man far removed from him. It seems Beowulf is not so much sad or bitter at the loneliness of his life, but perplexed by his death being such a lonely one.

Study Questions

1. How did Wiglaf come to own his armor?

2. Why does Wiglaf go to Beowulf's aid?

3. How is Beowulf mortally wounded?

4. How do the two men kill the dragon?

5. What is it Beowulf asks of Wiglaf after he is wounded?

6. When Wiglaf returns from fulfilling Beowulf's request, what further request is made of him by Beowulf?

7. What does Wiglaf say to Beowulf's followers when they return?

8. What is the message he sends with the herald to the people?

9. What is the Swedes' argument with the Geats?

10. What is it the warriors see that causes them to weep?

Answers

1. Wiglaf's family had once been Swedes. His father, Wexstan, served under Onela. At that time, Wexstan slew Onela's nephew after the nephew fled Sweden seeking safety with Herdred in Geatland. When Wexstan presented the nephew's weapons to Onela, they were returned to him. He, in turn, kept them for his son, Wiglaf, who inherited them upon his death. This battle with the dragon is the first time Wiglaf uses them.

2. Wiglaf goes to Beowulf's aid because he remembers how well his king had treated his family when they came to Geatland from Sweden. He is also grateful to Beowulf for choosing him as one of his warriors and realizes his king is now an old man—no matter how brave he is—and needs the help of his younger, stronger warriors.

3. As Wiglaf shouts words of encouragement to his lord, the dragon rushes him, breathing fire. When his wooden shield incinerates, Wiglaf jumps behind Beowulf's iron shield with him. Then the Geat king attacks the dragon with Nagling, which promptly breaks into pieces. The dragon is so enraged that he charges Beowulf, sinking his fangs into his neck and injecting his venom into Beowulf's body.

4. As the dragon assaults Beowulf, Wiglaf strikes its belly while Beowulf uses his dagger to split the dragon apart.

5. When he realizes he is mortally wounded, Beowulf asks Wiglaf to bring some of the treasure to him to ease his death.

6. Once Wiglaf returns from gathering the treasure, Beowulf asks him to become the leader of the Geats and, after his funeral, to build a high tower on the water's edge as Beowulf's tomb, so the sailors may see it and remember their king.

7. Wiglaf castigates Beowulf's followers as cowards and traitors for fleeing into the woods while their king fought the dragon. He blames them for their lord's death and says they would be better dead than living in the shame they must now endure for their cowardly behavior.

8. Wiglaf sends the message that both the dragon and their king are dead, and to beware of other countries attempting to start war with them once it is common knowledge the Geats no longer have a leader.

9. The Swedes' argument with the Geats stems from when their king, Ongentho, slew Hathcyn by waylaying him rather than engaging him in fair battle. He then allowed the Geats to begin looting, only to surround them, capture them, and taunt them the night through, fully intending to kill them

the next day. He was prevented from doing so by Higlac's arrival. Ongentho retreated, but was captured and brought to justice (as the Geats saw it).

10. The warriors weep after they pass the dragon's 50-foot corpse when they see their king's dead body laid out on the sand.

Suggested Essay Topics

1. Explore the possible reasons the dying Beowulf asks Wiglaf to bring him some of the dragon's treasures. Include in your discussion the custom of keeping a "souvenir" from a successful battle, and why Beowulf may have wanted to be able to give Wiglaf some of the treasure as a memento.

2. Wiglaf, in a sense, acts as Beowulf's heir. He is there when Beowulf dies; Beowulf asks him to be the next Geatish king; and Beowulf gives him some of the dragon's treasures. Discuss those values of Wiglaf's which may have caused Beowulf to recognize him as a good and noble warrior.

3. Pretending you are Wiglaf, explain why you feel you should stay with your lord and fight the dragon, even though all your fellow soldiers have fled for their lives.

Lines 3,058–3,182

Summary

Wiglaf carries out Beowulf's final instructions, explaining as he does so that Beowulf was worth far more than all of the gold and treasures, and that Beowulf should have left the dragon sleeping rather than risk the life that was so important to his people. Wiglaf leads seven of the noblest Geats past the treasure one last time to gather what they can of it in their arms to place on the funeral pyre with Beowulf. The dragon's corpse is rolled off the cliff into the sea, never to be seen again, while wood is gathered for the pyre. Once the pyre is built and the Geatish king's body placed upon it, surrounded by helmets and battle gear, the treasure is added. There is moaning and weeping as the pyre is ignited.

The Geats work for ten days on the tower near the sea to be used as Beowulf's tomb. His ashes are sealed within it, along with the treasure. Twelve of the bravest Geats ride around the tower, telling the stories of Beowulf's glory and of their own sorrow.

Analysis

Beowulf, a lonely man, strives for glory during his life, and at his death is remembered as a worthy man. Yet, it is a young man whom he had commanded who tells the people how to carry out Beowulf's final instructions. There is no wife, no child, no kinsman, no friend to do so. Beowulf led a successful life as far as his victories and the 50 years of his rule, but he led a solitary life, apparently not by choice since he mentions ruefully several times that he has neither son nor heir to whom he can leave his possessions.

While it is evident he led an exemplary life by Anglo-Saxon standards, and one to be emulated, modern standards lead the reader to believe his funeral and his passing were sad in more ways than one. Wiglaf uses the armor his father kept for him to defend a man he felt should not have risked his life to slay a dragon. But yet, Beowulf felt there was more glory in fame after death, and so, gave his life to kill the dragon. While Beowulf died as he chose, Wiglaf questions if this was a wise decision. His people are weeping, leaderless, and in danger of imminent attack as soon as their enemies hear of their leader's death. Was their king's decision made to save his people or for his own, solitary glory?

Study Questions

1. What does Wiglaf vainly attempt to tell Beowulf before he seeks the dragon?

2. According to Wiglaf, what are Beowulf's post-mortem instructions?

3. Who is to bring wood for Beowulf's funeral?

4. Why does Wiglaf bring the seven noblest Geats to the dragon's treasure?

5. What is done with the dragon's corpse?

6. How may the Geatish king's funeral pyre be described?

7. What do the Geats do as the fire is burning?

8. How long does it take to build the tomb Beowulf has asked for?

9. Why do 12 of the bravest Geats ride around the tower?

10. In the closing lines of the poem, how does the poet describe Beowulf?

Answers

1. Wiglaf vainly attempts to persuade his king to leave the dragon sleeping with his treasure, for it will be too costly for the Geats to lose their king and be left leaderless should the dragon be the victor in this battle.

2. Beowulf instructs Wiglaf that, after his death, his body should be burned and the ashes brought to the dragon's tower—which is to be made Beowulf's tomb.

3. Only the leaders of the Geatish people—the landowners, the bravest, the wealthiest—are to gather the wood for Beowulf's funeral.

4. The seven noblest Geats are brought to the treasure to gather from it what they can to place on Beowulf's funeral pyre, so that it may be burned along with his body.

5. The dragon's corpse is rolled off the cliff into the sea so that

it may never be seen again.

6. Beowulf's funeral pyre consists of his body and the treasure, surrounded by helmets and battle gear as Beowulf had requested.

7. While their king is being cremated, the Geats moan and lament his death. One old woman "groans" a song of misery for all of them.

8. It takes ten days for the Geats to make the tower tall and strong and seal both Beowulf's ashes and the dragon's treasure in this tomb.

9. Twelve of the bravest Geats ride around the tower to tell the stories of Beowulf's glory and also of their own mourning.

10. In the closing lines of the poem, the poet describes Beowulf as "beloved leader," the best king, the mildest prince, the man most open to his people, and "so deserving of praise."

Suggested Essay Topics

1. Beowulf died as he chose—in the fight with the dragon—yet Wiglaf seems to question if this was a wise decision, since the Geats are left leaderless and in danger of being attacked. Using evidence from the poem, do you agree with Wiglaf that Beowulf should have left the dragon alone?

2. Seven of the noblest Geats gather what they can of the treasure and place it on Beowulf's funeral pyre. What was the motive behind this action, since their leader had died in order to obtain that treasure for them?

Sample Analytical Paper Topics

These are topics on which you can write a substantial analytical paper. They are designed to test your understanding of major themes and details from the work as a whole. Following the topics are outlines you can use as a starting point for writing an analytical paper.

Topic #1

Beowulf, in his quest for glory, is reminiscent of a specific group of modern young executives who place their careers above all other aspects of their lives. How can this be validated from the poem?

Outline

I.   Thesis Statement: *In his single-minded quest for glory, Beowulf is reminiscent of a specific group of modern young executives in that they place their careers above all other aspects of their lives as he placed the quest for glory above all other aspects of his life.*

II.   Quest for glory

    A.   Slaying Grendel

    B.   Slaying Grendel's mother

    C.   Slaying the dragon

III.   Solitary life

    A.   Lack of wife

    B.   Lack of children

    C.   Lack of close friends

IV.   Military life

    A.   Travel at lord's orders

    B.   Live with other soldiers

    C.   Place lord over self

V.   Comparison with a specific group of modern young executives

    A.   Quest for great success quickly

    B.   Lack of social life or family life

    C.   Spend whatever little non-working time is available with co-workers

    D.   Place company values above personal values

Topic #2

The poem divides itself into three segments, each dealing with a different battle between Beowulf and a monster or dragon. Compare the three battles.

Outline

I.   Thesis Statement: *In his quest for glory, Beowulf fights three important battles—two with monsters and one with a dragon. These battles have both similarities and differences.*

II.   Battle with Grendel

    A.   Hrothgar sends for Beowulf

    B.   Grendel attacks Herot, killing Hondshew

    C.   Barehanded combat between Beowulf and Grendel

    D.   Beowulf kills Grendel by tearing off his claw, arm, and shoulder

    E.   Grendel escapes to his lair to die

III. Battle with Grendel's mother

    A. She attacks the sleeping Danes in Herot in revenge for the murder of her son

    B. The monster kills Esher, carrying off his body and her son's body parts

    C. Hrothgar's soldiers track her for Beowulf

    D. Barehanded battle until Beowulf uses the giants' magical sword which he finds in the battlehall

    E. Beowulf kills her by slicing into her neck

IV. Battle with the dragon

    A. Dragon awakened by thief/slave who steals a cup from his treasure

    B. Angry dragon uses his fiery breath to burn down the Geats' homes

    C. His own people summon Beowulf to slay the dragon

    D. Beowulf realizes he may die killing the dragon but battles him nonetheless

    E. Both Beowulf and the dragon are slain

Topic #3

Most of the poem deals with Beowulf's quest for glory. How is this detailed throughout the poem?

Outline

I. Thesis Statement: *Beowulf attempts to gain glory throughout his life.*

II. Early life

    A. Swimming contest with Brecca

    B. Chasing the giants from the earth

    C. Hunting monsters from the ocean

    D. War victories

III.   Battle with Grendel

    A.   Sails from Geatland to Denmark with a small band of soldiers specifically to kill the monster

    B.   Vows to fight barehanded

    C.   Wants to battle Grendel with only his small group of soldiers and no others

    D.   Prefers death to defeat

IV.   Battle with Grendel's mother

    A.   Promises Hrothgar he will kill her

    B.   Dons his armor and enters the lake alone

    C.   Keeps battling, despite the ineffectiveness of his weapons

    D.   Searches for Grendel's corpse after killing the mother monster

V.   Battle with the dragon

    A.   Intends to kill the dragon single-handedly

    B.   Uses an iron shield, sword, and armor only because of the dragon's fiery breath

    C.   Braves the heat of the dragon's fire

    D.   Calls the dragon with an angry battlecry

    E.   Dismembers the dragon even after incurring a mortal wound

Topic #4

The role of women was vastly different throughout history than it is today. Prove this from the poem.

Outline

I.   Thesis Statement: *Women's liberation and equality laws have greatly changed the role of women in society as can be seen through a reading of* Beowulf.

II.   Higd

   A.   Known as Higlac's queen

   B.   Sent gifts by Welthow, Hrothgar's queen

   C.   Served ale at her husband's banquets

   D.   Beowulf refuses the throne when she offers it to him, instead of her son, after her husband's death

III.   Welthow

   A.   Known as Hrothgar's queen

   B.   Serves mead at her husband's banquets

   C.   Speaks only to praise her lord

   D.   Expects Hrothulf to protect her sons upon her husband's death

   E.   Politically naive as demonstrated by her speech at the second feast wherein she claims all is at peace in Hrothgar's court

IV.   Finn's wife (no name given)

   A.   Finn attacks her people and kills their king

   B.   Her son and brother are killed in the battle

   C.   Her husband killed a year later at the end of the unwilling treaty Finn forced upon her people

   D.   Gratefully kidnapped by her people upon her husband's murder

Topic #5

The poem sung during the feast celebrating Beowulf's initial arrival at Herot is sometimes referred to as an "interior poem"—one which reflects the actual story and purpose of *Beowulf*. How is this evident?

Outline

I.   Thesis Statement: *The story of Siegmund, sung by the scop during the feast at Herot, in many ways reflects the actual story and purpose of* Beowulf.

II. Similarities between the story

   A. Both men are examples of heroic characters in pagan tradition

   B. Both men are involved in battle(s)

   C. Both men find treasure

   D. Both men are lauded after their death

III. The oral tradition in the song of Siegmund

   A. Certain ideas or phrases reiterated for emphasis

   B. Chosen to be appropriate to occasion at which it was recited

   C. Chosen with audience in mind—kings and nobles

   D. Reflects legends, myths, and histories with which audience would be familiar

   E. Reflects interests and values of culture at time it was told

IV. The oral tradition in *Beowulf*

   A. Certain ideas or phrases reiterated for emphasis

   B. Chosen to be appropriate to occasion at which it was recited

   C. Chosen with audience in mind

   D. Reflects legends, myths, and histories with which audience would be familiar

   E. Reflects interests and values of culture at time it was told

V.   Siegmund

   A. Heroic character

   B. Kills a dragon

    C.   Uses cunning as his main weapon in battle

    D.   Finds treasure

    E.   Final battle fought alone

VI. Beowulf

    A.   Heroic character

    B.   Kills two monsters and a dragon

    C.   Uses cunning as main weapon in battles

    D.   Finds treasure

    E.   Final battle fought alone

Appendix

The Language and Setting of *Beowulf*

Since *Beowulf* was written in Old English, any student studying this poem will be helped by learning something of the history of this language, and understanding the basic elements of Old English poetry.

According to most historians, the Anglo-Saxon period began in 449 and ended in 1066 with the Norman conquest. This was a period of 617 years, almost three times longer than America has been a country. From this period, only some 30,000 lines of poetry remain, about the length of a long best seller. Of this number, 3,182 lines comprise the poem *Beowulf.*

The Anglo-Saxon language reflects a history fraught with conquest and invasion. Prior to 449, there was already a great deal of conflict in the country. The Britons fought with the Celts, the Picts, and the Scots, even before the waves of invasions by the Romans, the Angles, the Saxons and the Jutes. Although the language retained some elements of these myriad cultures, it remained largely Germanic, sharing many aspects of Old High German, the language spoken in the homeland of the invaders.

Even within the Anglo-Saxon culture there was a great deal of diversity. The invaders settled in many kingdoms, separated by geographic boundaries and by the hostile British. Because of the isolation of each of these kingdoms, sound changes and tribal and individual peculiarities flourished in the different dialects. These

differences surfaced mainly in the spelling of various words. The language is frequently divided into four main dialects determined by geography. These are: Northumbrian, Mercian, West-Saxon, and Kentish. After the year 900, West-Saxon was increasingly used as the standard written language, and to this day, students learning Old English are commonly taught the spellings used by the West-Saxons.

Probably a large reason for the dominance of the language of the West-Saxons was that in the year 871 Alfred became ruler of their kingdom, by that point called "Wessex." Alfred came to be known as a more complex and forceful ruler than any previous king. He was both innovative and devoted to his subjects. To ensure a period of peace, he married his daughter to an ealdorman of Mercia, causing a strengthening alliance within the country which allowed him to more effectively protect his subjects from outside invaders. While his main objective was to ward off Danish invasions, he was also very concerned with the state of law, religion and education within his country.

Although there is no definitive proof, it is not unlikely that Alfred was the inspiration behind one of the longest surviving Anglo-Saxon texts—*The Anglo-Saxon Chronicle*. This is a historical account of the Anglo-Saxon history, beginning with the year 1 A.D. and the birth of Christ, and terminating in the year 1154 with the death of King Stephen. This represents the longest continuous record in Western History. The entries were recorded by monks, and told of battles, famines, monarchs, saints and religious leaders. They began as sparse entries of a sentence or two, but in later years, became extended and detailed descriptions of events. The *Chronicle* is remarkable in its use of the vernacular. The decline of the use of Latin in ninth century Britain made it necessary for Anglo-Saxon to become a written language, and began a process of refinement and sophistication of the language which would last until the Norman conquest.

Aside from *The Anglo-Saxon Chronicle*, Alfred is responsible for translations of biblical texts, treatises on the laws of the land, and other intellectually complicated writings. One notable work, reflecting the fact that during his reign the language became more commonly and more sophisticatedly written, explored his opinions on the necessity of education for his subjects, especially the teaching of writing and reading.

Alfred is one of the few authors of Anglo-Saxon literature about whom anything is known. Most of the work was anonymous, and much of it is quite mysterious and beautiful. Many unusual works, both of prose and of poetry, still survive to fascinate scholars. There are seven divisions of prose writing: The Anglo-Saxon chronicle; the translations of Alfred and his circle; homiletic writings; religious prose, including translations of the Old and New Testaments of the Bible; prose fiction; scientific and technical writings; and laws and charters. In the field of poetry, there are certain subjects which are commonly found: heroic subjects; historic poems; Biblical paraphrases; lives of the saints; other religious poems; short elegies and lyrics, and riddles and gnomic verse.

Closer examination of these poems reveals elements of Anglo-Saxon language usage that are unusual and very powerful. For instance, the riddles employ a practice of using the first person to speak for inanimate objects that helps to bring them alive. The subject of the riddle describes itself and asks to be identified. The answers of the riddle are frequently common, everyday things such as farm implements, items of food and drink, animals, insects, and weapons, helping to give a glimpse into the daily life of the Anglo-Saxons. For instance, one describes mead, one describes a swan, and another describes a one-eyed garlic peddler.

This method of personifying inanimate objects is expanded in one of the most unusual and beautiful of Old English poems, "The Dream of the Rood." The earliest dream-vision poem of the English language, this poem describes Christ's crucifixion and death on the cross from the point of view of the cross itself. By portraying Christ as a warrior-king, "The Dream of the Rood" represents a common trend in Anglo-Saxon literature: using the heroic diction of Old English to help make Christianity more acceptable to the Anglo-Saxons. The images used in the poem are strong and powerful such as the drops of blood from the cross congealing into beautiful gems and then turning back into blood once again.

Any discussion of Anglo-Saxon literature must begin with the understanding that it is, in fact, a completely different language from modern English, and that originally any manuscript in Anglo-Saxon required painstaking and complicated translation. There are even several letters in the Old English alphabet that no longer exist. These are: (æ) called "ash" and probably pronounced as we say the "a" in "hat"; and two letters (þ) called "thorn" and (ð) or (Ð) called "eth" which are both pronounced as "th" in "cloth" or "clothe".

Although the alphabet is different, the syntax of Anglo-Saxon is recognizably English. There are, however, several idiosyncrasies which add to the difficulty of translation. For one thing, Anglo-Saxon began as an inflected language, implying that the meaning of a sentence is determined by the case endings added to the beginnings and endings of words. In modern English, which is not an inflected language, meaning is determined for the most part by the order of words in a sentence. There are, however, some vestiges of inflection left in English as we use it today—the adding of "-s" or "-es" to make a word plural, for instance. The inflection in Old English is a direct product of its German ancestry. Throughout the course of its development, Old English became less and less inflected and word order became more important in determining meaning, and closer to what we recognize in our language today.

Another idiosyncrasy of syntax which adds to the difficulty of translation is the fact that Anglo-Saxon was originally mostly a spoken language. When King Alfred and his companions struggled to develop the language as a written vehicle for abstract thought and complex narratives, they utilized complicated patterns of words. These, coupled with erratic spelling and lack of punctuation, can cause the translation of Old English to be more like solving a puzzle or finding one's way out of a maze than translating from another language.

These complexities of language often affected the sentence structure. For instance, the author would frequently pause mid-sentence and start afresh with a group of words or a pronoun to summarize what had come before:

þa þæt Offan mæg   ærest onfunde,
þæt se eorl nolde   yrhðo geþolian [1]

---

1   Bruce Mitchell and Frederick C. Robinson, *A Guide to Old English* (Oxford: Basil Blackwell Ltd, 1988), p. 66.

This passage is translated as "Then the kinsman of Offa first learned that thing, that the leader would not tolerate slackness."[2] This device is probably used to stress an important idea in order to recapitulate what has been said, or to anticipate what is to be said.

Another practice which complicates translation of Old English is that of splitting groups of words which we would never consider splitting in modern English. To wit, two adjectives describing the same noun may come at different points in the sentence, divided by unrelated words. Or a subject containing two people or objects will be divided on either side of the verb. In modern English, this might result in a sentence such as, "I am going to work and my friend", rather than "My friend and I are going to work."

The vocabulary of Anglo-Saxon is extensive and imaginative, and it reflects the importance in the literature of strong, suggestive images. New words were acquired in three ways: borrowing from other languages, such as Latin, Greek, Scandinavian, or French; adding prefixes or suffixes which changed the function or meaning of the words; or making compounds of words. This last method—making compounds, resulted in some of the most imaginative and powerful images in the literature. Anglo-Saxon is typified by a unique brand of condensed metaphor, called a "kenning," in which (a) is compared to (b) without (a) or the point of comparison being made explicit. To illustrate, one word for "sea" was "hwæl-weg," which translates literally as "whale way," a ship was called a "yþ-hengest" or "whale horse," and a minstrel was a "hleahtor-smiþ" or "laughter smith."

These compounds helped the scop to work in alliterative measure. Because Anglo-Saxon poetry was originally oral rather than written, the poet had to rely on several different tricks to help himself remember the material. These kennings became like open patterns, different words could be replaced to change the meaning or work within a certain alliteration or rhythm.

The structure of the poems also functioned to help the poet tell his story. Poems are not in stanzaic form, nor do they usually intentionally rhyme. They are organized, rather, into two half-lines which have a natural pause between them. The sentences can con-

---

2   Mitchell and Robinson, *A Guide to Old English,* 61–62.

clude either at the middle or at the end of any given line. There is not a set number of syllables to be included in any half-line, although in *Beowulf* the average is eight to twelve per line. The half-lines are held together by alliteration, either of consonants or vowels.

The placement of the alliteration is determined by the stresses in the sentence. Each half-line has two strong stresses, the first stress of the second line (called the "head-stave") cannot alliterate with the second stress of that half-line, but must alliterate with one or both stressed syllables of the first half-line. All of these devices were part of an "oral-formulaic" system designed to help the poet remember his tale. There were many prefabricated half-lines or lines, designed to hold the tale together and give the poet time to think ahead.

The following section of *Beowulf*, describing his fight with the monster Grendel, demonstrates many of these patterns:

>   Cōm on wanre niht
> scrīðan sceadugenga.   Scēotend swǣfon,
> þā þæt hornreced   healdan scoldon –
> ealle būton ānum.   þæt wæs yldum cūþ,
> þæt hīe ne mōste,   þā metod nolde,
> se scynscaþa   under sceadu bregdan;
> ac hē wæccende   wrāþum on andan
> bād bolgenmōd   beadwa geþinges.
>   Ðā cōm of mōre   under misthleoþum
> Grendel gongan;   Godes yrre bær;
> mynte se mānscaða   manna cynnes
> sumne besyrwan   in sele þām hēan.
> Wōd under wolcnum   tō þæs þe hē wīnreced,
> goldsele gumena   gearwost wisse
> fǣttum fāhne.[3]

This passage translates as:

> He slipped through the darkness under deep nightfall
> sliding through shadows.   Shield-warriors rested

---

3   Mitchell and Robinson, *A Guide to Old English*, 268–269.

slumbering guardians   of that gabled hall—
all except one.   That wandering spirit
could never drag them   to cold death-shadow
if the world's Measurer   wished to stop him.
(A waking warrior   watched among them
anger mounting   aching for revenge.)
He moved through the mist   past moors and ice-streams
Grendel gliding   God's wrath on him
simmering to snare   some sleeping hall-thanes
trap some visitors   in that tall gift-house.
He moved under cloudbanks   crossed the meadowlands
till the wine-hall   towered tall gold-gables
rising in night-sky.[4]

Although this may seem very foreign to modern readers, it must be remembered that Old English poetry is far from primitive. It is highly sophisticated and artificial. This is sustained by the fact that the language used in poetry varies widely from that used in prose. This poetry differs from other types of poetry in that the metrical patterns are selected from among those which occur most commonly in natural speech. Perhaps this is part of what makes a recitation of Old English poetry such a moving and memorable occasion. The driving rhythm of the stresses, the beauty of the alliteration, the power of the subject matter and the vividness of the imagery combine to make the literature well worth the difficulties and complexities of translation.

---

4   Frederick C. Rebsamen, trans., *Beowulf: A Verse Translation* (New York: HarperCollins Publishers, 1991), p. 23.

SECTION SEVEN

Bibliography

Alexander, Michael, trans. & ed. *The Earliest English Poems.* New York: Penguin Books, 1966.

Bloom, Harold, ed. *Modern Critical Interpretations: Beowulf.* New York: Chelsea House Publishing, 1987.

Calder, Daniel G., ed. *Old English Poetry: Essays in Style.* California: University of California Press, 1979.

Chickering, Jr., Howell D., trans. *Beowulf: A Dual-Language Edition.* New York: Anchor Books, 1977.

Hieatt, Constance B., trans. *Beowulf and Other Old English Poems: Revised and Enlarged, Second Ed.* New York: Bantam Books, 1988.

Irving, Jr., Edward B. *Introduction to Beowulf.* New Jersey: Prentice-Hall, Inc., 1969.

Mitchell, Bruce and Frederick C. Robinson. *A Guide To Old English.* Oxford: Basil Blackwell Ltd, 1988.

Moulton, Charles Wells. *The Library of Literary Criticism of English and American Authors—Volume I (680 to 1,638).* Massachusetts: The Moulton Publishing Co., 1901.

Nist, John A. *The Structure and Texture of Beowulf.* Brazil: The Folcroft Press, 1959.

Ogilvy, J.D.A. & Baker, Donald C. *Reading Beowulf.* Oklahoma: University of Oklahoma Press, 1983.

Raffel, Burton. *Beowulf, A New Translation.* New York: The New American Library, 1963.

Rebsamen, Frederick, trans. *Beowulf: A Verse Translation.* New York: HarperCollins Publishers, 1991.

Savage, Anne, trans. and col. The Anglo-Saxon Chronicles. New York: St. Martins/Marek, 1983.

Trapp, J.B. *Medieval English Literature.* New York: Oxford University Press, 1973.

Tucker, Martin, gen. ed. *The Critical Temper from Old English to Shakespeare: A Survey of Modern Criticism on English and American Literature from the Beginning to the 20th Century—Volume I.* New York: Fredrick Unger Publishing Company, 1969.

Introducing...

MAXnotes
REA's Literature Study Guides

MAXnotes™ offer a fresh look at masterpieces of literature, presented in a live and interesting fashion. **MAXnotes**™ offer the essentials of what you should know about the work, including outlines, explanations and discussions of the ple character lists, analyses, and historical context. **MAXnotes**™ are designed to he you think independently about literary works by raising various issues and thoug provoking ideas and questions. Written by literary experts who currently teach t subject, **MAXnotes**™ enhance your understanding and enjoyment of the work.

Available **MAXnotes**™ include the following:

Animal Farm	The Great Gatsby	Moby-Dick
Beowulf	Hamlet	1984
Brave New World	Huckleberry Finn	Of Mice and Men
The Canterbury Tales	I Know Why the	The Odyssey
The Catcher in the Rye	Caged Bird Sings	Paradise Lost
The Crucible	The Iliad	Plato's Republic
Death of a Salesman	Julius Caesar	A Raisin in the Sun
Divine Comedy I-Inferno	King Lear	Romeo and Juliet
Gone with the Wind	Les Misérables	The Scarlet Letter
The Grapes of Wrath	Lord of the Flies	A Tale of Two Cities
Great Expectations	Macbeth	To Kill a Mockingbird

RESEARCH & EDUCATION ASSOCIATION
61 Ethel Road W. • Piscataway, New Jersey 08854
Phone: (908) 819-8880

Please send me more information about MAXnotes™.

Name _____

Address _____

City _____ State _____ Zip _____